The HOMEGIRL Devotional

by

Tensia Echols

Watersprings
PUBLISHING

The Homegirl Devotional by Tensia Echols
Published by Watersprings Publishing
P.O. Box 1284 Olive Branch, MS 38654
www.waterspringspublishing.com

Contact the publisher for bulk orders and permission requests.

Copyright © Tensia Echols. All rights reserved.

Scripture quotations credited to NIV are from the Holy Bible, New International Version. Copyright © 1973, 1978, 1984, 2011 by Biblica, Inc. Used by permission. All rights reserved worldwide.

Scripture quotations marked (NLT) are taken from the Holy Bible, New Living Translation, copyright © 1996. Used by permission of Tyndale House Publishers, Inc., Wheaton, IL 60189 USA. All rights reserved.

Scriptures marked HCSB are taken from the HOLMAN CHRISTIAN STANDARD BIBLE

(HCSB): Scripture taken from the HOLMAN CHRISTIAN STANDARD BIBLE, copyright© 1999, 2000, 2002, 2003 by Holman Bible Publishers, Nashville Tennessee. All rights reserved.

Scripture quotations marked AMP are taken from the Amplified Bible, New Testament Copyright © 1965, 1987, by the Zondervan Corporation. Used by permission. All rights reserved.

Scripture quotations marked "ESV" are taken from The Holy Bible, English Standard Version. Copyright © 2000; 2001 by Crossway Bibles, a division of Good News Publishers. Used by permission. All rights reserved.
Scripture quotations marked "NKJV" are taken from the New King James Version. Copyright © 1982 by Thomas Nelson, Inc. Used by permission. All rights reserved.

No part of this publication may be reproduced, distributed, or transmitted in any form or by any means, including photocopying, recording, or other electronic or mechanical methods, without the prior written permission of the publisher, except in the case of brief quotations embodied in critical reviews and certain other noncommercial uses permitted by copyright law.

Printed in the United States of America.

ISBN-13: 978-1-964972-10-7

The Homegirl Devotional

Introduction 5

Day 1: Girl Get Cozy 7

Day 2: BIG Faith 9

Day 3: His Promise > Your Preference. 12

Day 4: He Did It, You Don't Have To 14

Day 5: In You, I Am Strong 17

Day 6: Change Your Mind, Change Your Life 20

Day 7: Master Peace 23

Day 8: Pop Quiz 27

Day 9: For Purpose, On Purpose 30

Day 10: Simple Life 33

Day 11: Don't Look Back. 36

Day 12: Humility Looks Good On You 39

Day 13: Wife-Like 42

Day 14: Watch Your Mouth 45

Day 15: Get Ready. Get Set. Believe. 48

Day 16: What's the Real? 51

Day 17: Control Freak 54

Day 18: Spirit Animal 57

Day 19: Compare? Beware! 60

Day 20: Troubleshoot 66

Day 21: Power Struggle 67

Day 22: Not Perfect, But Patient 69

Day 23: Sheep's Clothing 71

Day 24: Flee From Me 73

Day 25: Daddy's Girl 76

Day 26: Gatekeeping 78

Day 27: Empty Tomb 80

Day 28: Restful Thinking 82

Day 29: Holy Boldness 86

Day 30: No Gray 89

Day 31: Less of Me 92

About the Author 99

Introduction

To be intimate with someone or something is to be closely acquainted, familiar, close, private, personal, and friendly. Unfortunately, I feel as though intimacy has been misinterpreted, perverted even, in a way that we would never comfortably use, pertaining to our relationship with The Lord. In a world that takes our delicate hearts and mishandles them with false truths on the everyday images on TV, a daily scroll on social media, maybe even a public encounter, and for some of us, a church service. I wrote this devotional for the woman seeking understanding and to be understood. I wrote this for the woman trying to find herself in God and find God in herself.

I wrote this devotional for the woman who is ready for a fresh perspective, a new perspective, or just a perspective period of God and the many ways of His unconditional love, unmerited favor, and unconditional grace. I also found it imperative to include scriptural references throughout because my desire is to lead you to an authentic, Earth-shattering transformation, and that only happens when we open the word of God for ourselves and allow His word to attack our hearts. I believe heavily that the Word of God is the foundation of the life that God desires for us, but we have to come to know it for ourselves!

Also, after each reading for the day, you will experience the application of God's word working in you through ***prayer*** in agreement with the Word of God, ***pushing*** yourself to answer some questions about yourself that will create a safe and vulnerable space with God. Daily ***praise reports*** will present a chance to honor God and give Him glory; lastly, through ***proclamation***, which is an out-loud agreement with God to pursue His Word and claim it to be true in your life. Additionally, after each week, there's a page to write your "Homegirl Notes," to jot down anything that's important to you, or journal your thoughts for deeper reflection.

So, for the next 31 days, I pray that you can create an intimate and sacred space in your heart for God because that is precisely where God wants to be with you! Every day, I pray that you create a time to snuggle up in the comfort of God's peace, find safety in vulnerability, and dissect these pages, allowing true revelation to come through what God is about to do in and through you.

Let's pray, *"Dear God, open my heart and help me find my safe space in You! Through this devotional, I want to learn more about You, be sensitive to Your voice, and be obedient to Your word. I love You and am excited about this new journey with You. In Jesus' name, amen."*

Day 1

Girl Get Cozy

"But when you pray, go into your room, close the door and pray to your father, who is unseen. Then your father, who sees (what is done) in secret, will reward you."
Matthew 6:6 AMP

Do you ever feel like God doesn't recognize or acknowledge your prayers? The gut-wrenching feeling of self-doubt or disbelief that utters, "God doesn't hear me." "Why would He listen to me?" It's hard not to think this way because having intimate conversations with tangible people is hard enough, but having faith in what we can't see and struggle to hear can sometimes seem impossible. I believe God just wants us to trust and try. It is reassuring to know that God loves talking to you so much that sometimes He just wants it to be you and Him. No theatrics, no crowd, no perfect performance, nor the perfect words to say! Nope, just you, your heart, and an amazing Heavenly Father, who is waiting to reward the obedience of your truth with His presence and peace.

"But in my distress I cried out to the Lord; yes, I prayed to my God for help. He heard me from his sanctuary; my cry to him reached his ears." Psalms 18:6 NLT

With the help of this devotional, I pray that you find your sacred space with God, remove the spiritual makeup, and allow God to see the natural beauty of who you are as He guides you to the woman you're steadily becoming.

Pray:

"God, thank you so much for Your gentle reminder that You hear me and desire to spend time with me. Please create in me the desire to spend time with You, the discipline to do it frequently, and the discernment to know Your voice. In Jesus' name. Amen."

Push:

1. What keeps you from making prayer a practice?
1. How can you make prayer a prerequisite to your relationship with the Lord?

Praise Report:

Describe a time when you vividly remember being in the midst of an answered prayer. Honor God for being a God who hears His daughter.

Proclaim:

"I will prepare to be the woman God has called me to be through fervent prayer and petition, making prayer a priority every day of my life."

Day 2

BIG Faith

If that is how God clothes the grass of the field, which is here today and tomorrow is thrown into the fire, will he not much more clothe you- you of little faith?
Matthew 6:30 NIV

You remember being younger and wanting to go to your favorite restaurant for dessert or your favorite person's house to have fun, and mom or dad said you could go? Then time rolls by, and you circle back to remind them, "Hey, you said…" We soaked in the satisfaction of remembering what they said, believing what they said, and wanting it to come to pass, so much so that we had enough guts to remind them! The only reason we go back to remind them, and even sometimes more than once, is because we genuinely believe what they say and have faith that they'll do it. We have this faith in earthly parents but struggle to have this same faith and belief in God. It's impossible to have faith in a word we don't believe to be true.

"And without faith it is impossible to please him, for whoever would draw near to God must believe that he exists and that he rewards those who seek him." Hebrews 11:6 ESV

We should be constantly reading our Word so that we can have the faith to bring God's Word back to Him! Our petitioning of God should start first with BELIEF in who He is and, secondly, BELIEF in His Word. God desires for us to have enough faith and belief in His Word to not only read, receive, and live by it but also to bring it back to Him! There's nothing wrong with reminding our Heavenly Father of His Word. The Bible tells us that we serve a never-changing God. Therefore, His word can't and won't change either, however, we can't remind Him of what we don't know or fail to believe ourselves.

"The grass withers and the flowers fade, but the word of our God stands forever." Isaiah 40:8 NLT

Pray while reading your Word that the words be made real in your mind and heart so that you can experience how they undoubtedly affect your relationship with God. The only variable in the relationship between you and God is you! God hasn't changed, and in better news, He never will!

"For I am the Lord, I do not change [but remain faithful to my covenant with you]... Malachi 3:6 NKJV

It has to be your decision to change the practiced prayer into a proper petition and infrequent reading of scripture into devoted time in your Word! That's the key to "big faith!"

Pray:

"God, sometimes, I struggle with practicing prayer out of habit and obligation. I never want prayer to feel like a chore. I pray against doubt and disbelief! I choose to get to know You better by first believing that Your Word is true and that You are never changing. I'm excited about my journey to "BIG Faith," but I can't do it without you. I choose to trust You. In Jesus' name. Amen."

Push:

1. Do you make reading/studying the Bible an actual practice in your faith?

2. What challenges do you face when trying to or actually reading the Word of God?

Praise Report:

Describe the revelation you received from reading the Word of God this week. How did it bring clarity to your walk with the Lord?

Proclaim:

"I am made confident in my faith by reading the Word of God, and there I will see His Glory, and my faith will be renewed."

Day 3

His Promise > Your Preference

I will instruct you and teach you in the way you should go; I will counsel you (who are willing to learn) with my eye upon you.
Psalm 32:8 NIV

Abraham was indeed braver than most of us. The Bible tells us that God instructed Abram to go where he would tell him to go. *"The Lord had said to Abram, "Leave your native country, your relatives, and your father's family, and go to the land that I will show you."* Genesis 12:1 NLT

Most of us would have stopped listening at leaving the country. Like, ok, God, maybe city, but country? You're pushing it. Others of us would've stopped at our family. Like no God, not my home and safe place. Who will come when I need them? The best and scariest part was that he didn't even give Abraham the final destination. God wanted him to trust His promise over his preferences. Imagine if Abram didn't go. We wouldn't be blessed today because he chose what he preferred to do over what God promised to do in his obedience. Truth is, your preference isn't so promising. I know that we are living in a time where culture makes life all about "your wants, your needs, and your happiness." However, life isn't only about you, and it isn't supposed to be. Your preferred way of doing a thing, "just being this way" or simply just not wanting to, can be holding not only you back but those who God entrusted in your proximity to bless by your obedience. It should ignite you to know that your Heavenly Father longs for you to trust Him so that He can grant you the guide-map to your life and fulfill the predestined purpose that He has for you. He has already gone before you to protect you just as He did Abraham, *"You will not leave in a hurry, running for your lives. For the Lord will go ahead of you; yes, the God of Israel will protect you from behind."* Isaiah 52:12 NLT

He loves you enough to go again with you, while counseling you through, if you allow God to do through you what He has already instilled in you.

Pray:

"God, thank You so much for having a predestined promise for my life. I struggle with putting what I prefer over the ways that You've patiently shown me. Help me to walk humbly in being gracefully counseled by You and to make Your promise, my preference. In Jesus' name. Amen."

Push:

1. List three preferences that potentially keep you from your promise from God. (Don't hold back!)
2. How can you adopt God's Word into your heart so that your preferences become a reflection of His promise?

Praise Report:

How has God changed your preferences since getting to know Him better?

Proclaim:

"I prefer God's promise over my preference because, in His presence, all things are made new."

Day 4

He Did It, You Don't Have To

"I have told you all this so that you may have peace in me. Here on Earth you will have many trials and sorrows, but take heart, I have overcome the world."
John 16:33 NLT

To take heart is to take comfort or confidence in something; if we have to take heart in anything, Jesus is the perfect place to do so. The *Earth*, that we jokingly to refer to as "ghetto," Jesus came here, yes here! Not because He was eager to see what it was like but because He was eager to save us from ourselves so that we could come to know God in a way that would help us have peace in everyday life.

"Jesus told him, "I am the way, the truth, and the life. No one can come to the Father except through me." John 14:6 NLT

It is through Jesus that we experience His grace, which is unfathomable and incomprehensible. It is through Jesus that we can commune with God, and He communes with us. It is through Jesus that we are released through the gift of repentance. Prayerfully, you've had time to come face to face with things to take to God in prayer. It is my hope that you leave all of the things that concern you, worry you, keep you up at night, and potentially trouble you right there!

> *"Don't worry about anything; instead, pray about everything. Tell God what you need and thank him for all he has done."*
> *Philippians 4:6 NLT*

Why? Because leaving our problems provides true comfort, and being redirected in our path from the gift of repentance is freeing. If we begin to take Jesus at His Word, we will experience true confidence in Him and know that there is nothing in this world that He has not already experienced and defeated on our behalf. Although it is no shock to God that we face the trials, the trauma, and the tribulations, He took it all and put it on Jesus's back. And out of the unfathomable love that He has for you, allowed Jesus to pay the cost so that you could experience the life-changing experience of knowing and having a relationship with Him. God paid it forward in a way that we can hardly fathom. It is your job to walk in the wealth, show to yourself that you are a great investment, and trust that He freed you from sin, and He sees you now through the eyes of our savior!

Pray:

"God, thank you for declaring my worth before I even knew it. You sent Your perfect Son to die for my imperfections. And yet, when my mess shows its face, You've proved that You're there to clean, correct, convict, and comfort me all over again. You are the best Father that I could ever ask for. I get to snuggle in Your abundant love, unfathomable grace, and perfect peace! I love You, God! Forever and ever, Amen.

Push:

1. Do you allow your sin to be a weight in your life that attempts to keep you down or hold you back?

2. How can you begin to trust Jesus to be your true Anchor and turn away from the things trying to keep you down?

Praise Report:

What is one weight or sin that you have recently been freed from that will bring you freedom and glory to God?

Proclaim:

> *"I will take heart in Jesus in this life and no longer walk with the weight of sin. God sees me as worthy, and I am redeemed."*

Day 5

In You, I Am Strong

So I am well pleased with weaknesses, with insults, with distresses, with persecutions and with difficulties, for the sake of Christ; for when I am weak (In Human Strength), then I am strong (truly able, truly powerful, truly drawing from God's strength.)
2 Corinthians 12:10 AMP

"Strength" is such a celebrated term. Everyone wants to be strong. It seems so admirable. Physical strength. Mental strength. All so good, seemingly so beneficial. And it really can be until it becomes artificial. The desire to uphold weight that is causing you to be completely torn down is not true strength. If you are anything like me, when you feel an utterance, even an inkling of defeat or weakness, you try your best to "defeat defeat" or outwork "weakness." You work, work, work, trying to prove a point or outdo yourself to prove to you and whoever else that "you got it," and that "you are so strong," or "you can do it all."

Then, it becomes even more of a self-diagnosed expectation because people around you can begin to label you as "the one who has it all together" or "strong one." We can even unknowingly create a more dangerous space by seeking the praise and approval of others because now we have attached it to our identity and feel the need to be this way for others all of the time. Truthfully, I am so proud of you for being such a strong and independent woman, but God wants you to know it is OK not to ALWAYS be strong. We don't have to be the strength for the next person or even ourselves. Our strength should be uniquely in loving and relying on God because He is our true source. Not us!

"I love you, Lord; you are my strength." Psalms 18:1 NLT

God wants to show Himself clearly in your life if you allow more of the weak moments. What if I told you that weakness is sometimes worth it? Because in it, God is working!

"Then Jesus said, "Come to me, all of you who are weary and carry heavy burdens, and I will give you rest."
Matthew 11:28 NLT

Give God a chance to lighten the load. I'm sure You think you got it, but never forget that God has you! God desires to decrease the weight if you're willing to wait on Him.

Pray:

"Thank You, God, for Your desire to lighten the load! It is heavy often, but You never designed for me to carry it all. In You, I can brag about not being able to do it all because You love me enough to cover me. Please help me in my humility so that I am able to identify each moment, surrender it to You, and rest in the peace that comes with the strength You give me in Jesus' name, amen."

Push:

1. What event in your life created a sense of self-reliant strength in you?
2. How can you create a space for weakness in your life so that God can show His strength in and through you?

Praise Report:

Describe a moment where you know that it was God's strength that brought you through a situation that your human strength could not.

Proclaim:

"I am confident in God's ability to work through my weakness. It is through my weakness that I experience the full strength of the Lord."

Day 6

Change Your Mind, Change Your Life

Do not conform to the patterns of this world, but be transformed by the renewing of your mind. Then you will be able to test and approve what God's will is- His good, pleasing and perfect will.
Romans 12:2 NIV

I don't think anybody was more fitting than Paul to be the author of such a divine truth in our everyday faith. Although miraculous changes took place in the Holy Bible, Gangsta Paul most certainly made a radical one. A persecutor and slayer of Believers turned one of the loudest and proudest Disciples to share the Gospel! Wow! Meanwhile, we often put ourselves to shame for sins that God has already forgiven, allowing them to be the barrier between our now and our next.

What sins have overtaken your thoughts so much that you don't believe in the freedom that has already been assigned to you? Our thoughts have the power to assassinate our assignment if we allow them to. I think it's only right that you stop now and pray for the strength to bring it to God, then trust in him for the strength to turn away from it.

"Finally, brothers and sisters, whatever is true, whatever is noble, whatever is right, whatever is pure, whatever is lovely, whatever is admirable—if anything is excellent or praiseworthy—think about such things."
Philippians 4:8 NIV

You may hear quite often that it is our thoughts that control our actions. It's very realistic to hear something so often that your mind writes it off as a rehearsed saying versus an impactful truth to life. The truth of the matter is that every action that we do or do not perform all starts with the way we think about it first! I believe that this is emphasized in Romans because oftentimes, we attempt to go at faith with a potentially warped view of our Lord and Savior, Jesus Christ. May I submit that real mind renewal comes with truly knowing and believing God's word? If we actually come out of our thoughts for a moment to adopt the thoughts and ways of God in pursuit of believing them to be true about ourselves, we would walk victoriously in all the things he has called us out of and boldly in the things he has called us into. Today, God has given you the strength to choose to allow your mind to be renewed with the never-changing truth of His word! Feelings will always pay a visit, but the word of God can live in you and evict the visitor of lies every single time!

Pray:

"Dear God, thank You for Your Word. I never noticed how much Your Word helped me through everyday feelings that try to haunt me. I want my mind to be renewed, not with the media and the ways of today's culture, but with the ways of Christ. Create in my heart a home for Your Word so that lies can't stay. My mind is made new in You. In Jesus' name. Amen."

Push:

1. Why do you think God chose Paul to be one of Jesus's strongest disciples and sharers of the Gospel, given his prior lifestyle?

2. What constant thoughts do you have of yourself that block you from believing in who God has called you to be? What truth of God can you adopt in your heart to replace those thoughts with?

Praise report:

Share where you are now in your faith as a testament to God's goodness and the mind shift that occurred in you.

Proclaim:

"I will spend more time in the Word of God so that my life reflects how my mind has been renewed."

Day 7

Master Peace

"Then you will experience God's peace, which exceeds anything we can understand. His peace will guard your hearts and minds as you live in Christ Jesus."
Philippians 4:7 NLT

If you had a dollar for every time you found yourself worrying about something, you surely wouldn't be worried about your finances. You could be thinking, "Nah" I don't really worry too much, but I bet you allow the things you "don't worry" about to cross your mind at least once a day. It is a normal and expected reaction to the things that take place in our day-to-day lives. The behavior of our children or the hopes to have them, an ill family member, a troubled marriage, or hopes to be married soon, finances, careers, and futures, to name a few. One of the many names of God is Jehovah Jireh, our provider! And often, when we hear "provision," we immediately think of finances. However, God is a provider of all things good, and it is my prayer that you petition Him and trust Him to be the provider of your peace.

"For He is our peace, who made both one…" Ephesians 2:14

It's one thing for the situation to shift, and certainly nothing wrong with praying for that shift to happen, but it's another thing to be in the thick of it and have peace to sleep in a storm and command it to be still like our savior did in the book of Mark. (Mark 4:39) We, although sometimes hard to believe, have that same power living on the inside of us.

"The Spirit of God, who raised Jesus from the dead, lives in you. (And just as God raised Christ Jesus from the dead, he will give life to your mortal bodies by this same Spirit living within you."
Romans 8:11 NLT

Worrying, stressing, and overthinking about things can leave us leaning on our own understanding and attempting to make sense of it all for ourselves. God doesn't want that for you. Instead, He says in Philippians 4:6, He wants you to not worry but pray. It's definitely easier said than done to leave the overthought thoughts, stressors, and worries behind us, but if we trust God enough to replace panic with praise, He will turn the panic into peace. A peace that surpasses understanding transcends the place we're in and gives us the holy boldness to trust God more than ourselves.

Pray:

"God, thank You for being the Master of peace. It's not always easy to have peace in situations because life brings about some tough challenges, but in all of that, You have kept me, and You are so faithful. Give me the tenacity to replace my panic with praise and accept the peace that comes with knowing and trusting You. I desire to have peace in every place that I'm in, and with You, I know that I can. In Jesus' name, amen."

Push:

1. What in your life is currently keeping you from the peace that God desires for you to experience?

2. What can you implement in your daily life that will help you overcome overthinking and stress?

Praise Report:

Describe a current or past situation where you experienced the unexplainable peace of God in a not-so-peaceful situation.

Proclaim:

"Dear Lord, I will not continue to allow my overthinking to justify praising the problems. I will praise You and reap in peace as You receive the glory, as Your will is done in my life."

Homegirl Notes

Day 8

Pop Quiz

"Be assured that the testing of your faith [through experience] produces endurance [leading to spiritual maturity, and inner peace]."
James 1:3 AMP

Do you remember when the year "2022" was ending and "2023" was beginning, and the trending thing was to "not become one of God's strongest soldiers?" I'm pretty sure that everyone wanted to get in on that request! The truth of the matter is that the tests we encounter day to day can be so challenging that they can begin to feel more like a pop quiz! You know, the surprise test from the teacher whose class is already not easy! However, despite its difficulties, the test typically depends on information that we've discussed, taken notes on, or have been dealing with for some time. That's exactly how the test can be in our faith. The test of life may feel like a surprise in the midst, but everything we've been through should have prepared us, sharpened our faith, built endurance in us, and allowed spiritual maturity to come forth out of us. The difference between God and the not-so-easy schoolteacher is that we don't have to take the test quietly, with a closed book, or alone. God wants us to talk to him through every moment and, contrary to false belief, even ask questions. We're reminded of this in Isaiah 41:10, *"Don't be afraid, for I am with you. Don't be discouraged, for I am your God. I will strengthen you and help you. I will hold you up with my victorious right hand."*

Thankfully, our books can be open; the best book, the Holy Bible, guides us to the correct way of answering life's issues, and once we allow the word in us, we surely won't feel alone because we will be assured that God is with us. God doesn't expect us to have the correct answers on our own so that we receive a perfect score! In fact, there is no perfect score, and He is the answer. His patience, His grace, and His mercy! So, in the different tests of life, we get to stand strong on the faith that was built in previous seasons and endure in spiritual maturity with our Lord with us, Emmanuel, every step of the way.

Pray:

"God, thank You for the tests that I have been given, and thank You for giving me all the answers I need to get through them. I truly wouldn't have gotten this far in life if it wasn't for Your grace and love. Help me not to endure the test grudgingly but gracefully because of the spiritual maturity that it builds in me. The tests may not be the easiest, but they always get easier with You. In Jesus' name, amen."

Push:

1. What is one of the hardest tests that God brought you through that made you realize you had some spiritual maturing to do?

2. How can you change your perspective on the next test of life so that you gain spiritual maturity and endure the next season?

Praise Report:

Recall a time when you may have had a test you were ill-prepared for but passed anyway. In the same way, the Lord will refresh your mind for a time such as that. He does that and so much more with the guidance of the Holy Spirit in our everyday lives.

Proclaim:

"I will not be shaken by the next tests that come for my faith, for my faith is my foundation as I grow in spiritual maturity and endurance. I stand firm on the word of God."

Day 9

For Purpose, On Purpose

"And we know that God causes everything to work together for the good of those who love God and are called according to his purpose for them."
Romans 8:28 NLT

I know that purpose is such a heavy topic because everyone wants to know, "What is MY purpose?" The "purpose" industry in today's time is a million-dollar industry all to try to sell a person by informing them of what they should be doing in life and with their life despite God's already word over our lives. Trust me, I get it; I, too, have fallen victim many times, concerning myself with this very question and not knowing what's next. No one wants to feel as though they are just here, day by day, showing up with no sense of fulfillment. The truth is, you desire to make an impact somehow; someway, everybody does. Even for the one who is found in the corner of the room and feels invisible, you would rather be confident and walk into the room knowing exactly who you are and whose you are. The good news is that God is an extremely intentional God, and in His intentionality, He skillfully, wonderfully, and patiently created you. For purpose. On purpose. Question for you, though: do you love God? Like really love God? Because if we did the way we proclaim, the purpose pursuit wouldn't be such a driving force to our why, but our love for God would. Scripture tells us that He is working for the good of us who love him! If your answer is yes, could you exercise loving Him a little more? He loves you so much He couldn't just stop at words. Instead, He sacrificed His only son to be closer to you.

"Christ suffered for our sins once for all time. He never sinned, but he died for sinners to bring you safely home to God." 1 Peter 3:18

The Lord desires to make everything in your life work for the good of you and to ultimately bring glory to His name. Everything you may have written off or even tried to ignore feeds into the exact reason that you are here. So, our first steps to discovering the million-dollar 'purpose pursuit' are not in the next self-help book or the popular podcast. It starts with loving God! Wholeheartedly and unadulterated. In spirit and in truth, and from that love, the one who knows exactly why the Earth needed YOU will guide you in the exact purpose that He has called you to.

Pray:

"God, I will admit I have been searching for my purpose outside of You sometimes. I didn't know it was as simple as loving You authentically! Please help me to love You the way that You love me. I trust You, the Creator of life, to purposefully guide me in mine. I will love You and allow You to lead me. In Jesus' name. Amen."

Push:

1. Do you struggle with not feeling purposeful?
2. How can you act on your love for God more in your personal life so that you can experience the will of God for your life?

Praise Report:

Praise God for showing you His will for your life, and thank Him for considering you to be the answer to that problem in the world.

Proclaim:

"I was created for purpose on purpose, skillful and wonderfully, and I will open my heart to the Lord so that I can walk in His will for my life."

Day 10

Simple Life

"Jesus told them, "This is the only work God wants from you: Believe in the one he has sent."
John 6:29 NLT

Work can suck! At least HAVING to work does. Even in the event of loving your work, sometimes, just sometimes, we need a break! In the event that you are not "clocking in," to a job site, there's something that we do, almost daily, that would essentially contribute to our well-being and how we live our lives. I think what makes work the least enjoyable is the constant discipline that it requires. Consistency around the house, alarm clocks, schedules, meetings, phone calls, reports, bookings, and the list goes on! The fact is, with whatever work we do, we have to put something in to receive anything out of it. I would like to argue that in that way, our relationship with the Lord is very similar. It takes work and effort and requires some discipline, But the reward is far worth it and so much greater. If we actually put our faith and trust in the Lord, our reward is a simple life. God suggests we do one thing as it pertains to "work." And that is to believe. Believe in who He sent! Now, why would that be the work that God requires, one could ask? It's simply because the belief in our Savior truly sets the framework for our day-to-day lives. With our belief in Jesus, our foundation is secure, and there's nothing within the agreement of God that is out of our reach or impossible for us to attain and/or do.

"Delight yourself in the Lord, And He will give you the desires and petitions of your heart." – Psalm 37:4

Our belief in the Lord creates fruit in our hearts that is foundational to our relationships with people. Belief produces faith that allows a fullness and fulfillment that can only come from Him. It is Jesus, our Lord, who fills us with daily bread so that we may never grow hungry and quenches our thirst so that we may never thirst again.

"Jesus replied, "I am the bread of life. Whoever comes to me will never be hungry again. Whoever believes in me will never be thirsty." - John 6:35

There will never be enough work that we can do that will set us up for a better life than believing in our true sustainer. Not saying that bills don't have to be paid, but I am saying that the ultimate price for your freedom and salvation was already taken care of. Therefore, our belief in Jesus is well worth the discipline required for the simple life it allows us to live.

Pray:

"God, I can admit that sometimes I struggle with the concept of believing and allowing Jesus to fill me up. I can complicate life by filling myself with things that aren't substantial, so I then feel empty again. Help me to understand that You fill every void, supply every need, and secure me in every way. Help me to have faith in this simple life with You versus the hard life that I can sometimes create for myself. In Jesus' name. Amen."

Push:

1. What does a simple life look like to you? Describe.

2. Do you believe that trusting in the Lord will give you peace that will help you to live life more simply?

Praise Report:

Pause. Take a deep breath. In this moment of clarity, thank God for desiring a simpler life for you and for gifting us a Savior who has made this possible.

Proclaim:

"I live life with the belief in the Lord as my foundation; therefore, my life has been made simple."

Day 11

Don't Look Back

"...Run for your lives! And don't look back or stop anywhere in the valley! Escape to the mountains, or you will be swept away!"
Genesis 19:17 NET

Ok, seriously, the past hosts some good moments and memories! I mean, everyone has at least one "Boy, we had a time" flashback, right? And maybe your flashback was just yesterday. Either way, it troubles me to wonder, does that flashback reveal more of who you are or the woman that you're steadily becoming? I believe that it is in our best interest not to mourn the things behind us, allowing what we consider the "good times" to go versus the popular and typically preferred "letting them roll." Our definitions of good or fun are oftentimes not in alignment with what God would consider good or fun if we aren't in alignment with Him. May I submit a challenge to you to let go of the life that could potentially be in the shadows and live a life that happily embraces being set apart? Now, allow me to provide further clarity. A set-apart life should not be associated with boring, although I know that it could be without context. A set-apart life is simply better, blessed, and abundant. It is better because it allows us to live more confidently and less convicted. Blessed because we are no longer only known by God, but now have allowed desire to grow in our hearts to come to know Him for ourselves. And abundantly, because God doesn't run out of anything, so the time we spend in His presence allows us to receive all of the good that God intended for us.

"For we are God's masterpiece. He has created us anew in Christ Jesus, so we can do the good things he planned for us long ago."
Ephesians 2:10

Listen, the Lord is kind and truly wants you to enjoy yourself in this life, but in the parameters that He set to protect you! Maybe, for you, this looks like replacing the club or wild party with dinner and genuine laughs with friends. Or even replacing the sneaky link with someone who sees you and desires to be seen with you. Maybe even the substance that provides a false sense of comfort for the Savior whose comfort is without question and never leaving. Whatever it is, every good thing isn't always God; however, God is always good!

Pray:

"God, I sometimes think that following You means leaving what I consider fun behind. Please change how I think so I can fully embrace life with You. I want to experience Your love for me fully and abundantly, and I know I can't do this if I keep clinging to things that don't align with Your promise for my life. I want to be new, but I need the strength that comes from You. In Jesus' name. Amen."

Push:

1. Do you have an area of your life that you try to keep God away from? Why?
2. How can you surrender that to God so that you can live a set-apart life that glorifies Him?

Praise Report:

Thank God for freeing you from secrecy, allowing you to be transparent with Him, and not ashamed of your ability to surrender to our Savior.

Proclaim:

"I am free from anything that attempts to separate me from an honest life with the Lord. There is nothing I want to keep from Him!"

Day 12

Humility Looks Good On You

"So humble yourselves under the mighty power of God, and at the right time he will lift you up in honor."
1 Peter 5:6 NLT

To be humble is to be free from pride or arrogance, which is a low view of one's own importance. In contrast, today, we celebrate everything pertaining to ourselves. Everything has been made to be self-seeking, self-centered, and plainly selfish. Although there are most certainly times in life when there is a need for some self-focus because one can simply not pour from an empty cup, we have to be cautious of what our time to ourselves looks like. Is it a moment of isolation in arrogance or a moment of separation in wisdom? I know that this may not be the most appealing thing you've ever read, especially in times like today, where you've actually read and heard the exact opposite of this exactly, but it should be our reality. Self-made, self-happiness, and self-reliance have been quoted and paraded around for us to adopt into our belief system as though God is truly not the reason and the source of all things we desire to attain. It is impossible to experience the fullness of God if you think your self-relevance is most important in the relationship. (Ephesians 3:19)

As women, we can sometimes disguise a "God complex" as independence and wonder why we're not hearing or experiencing God. We then become unable to process the voice of God because we download too many lies that don't agree with His word. We begin to think that our success comes through acts of hard work and self-sufficiency vs. the provision of God. (James 1:17)

Humility isn't something God does for you but something you have enough reverence for God to do yourself. Independence is beautiful, but humility is breathtaking. If you sit at God's feet long enough, He will appoint you to the right seat at the right time! So be patient gorgeous grasshopper, God sees you, He is waiting on you to see less of you and more of Him.

Pray:

Dear God, thank You for leaving humility up to me. Being humbled is not fun and can be a bit embarrassing. I can sometimes allow the confidence or lack thereof to become an idol in my life, and I forget that it is You who deserves all of the glory. Help me with self-awareness in moments where I should be meek and allow You to speak through me. Forgive me for the times that I have been arrogant to think that I am behind all good things when it is indeed You. Thank You for seeing me and helping me to see more of You, in Jesus' name.

Push:

1. Do you struggle with self-righteousness (having or being characterized by a certainty, especially an unfounded one, that one is totally correct or moral)?

2. Do you believe that all good things come from God and that HE is Jehovah Jireh, our provider?

Praise Report:

Offer the Lord the fruit of your lips with praise and thanksgiving for all He is doing and has done for you! Thank Him for not having to do it all alone.

Proclaim:

> *"When I look in the mirror, I am beginning to see less of me and more of Jesus. Humility looks good on me."*

Day 13

Wife-Life

> *"A worthy wife is a crown for her husband, but a disgraceful woman is like cancer in his bones."*
> *Proverbs 12:4 NLT*

Let me tell you, "wife" isn't the easiest role or title in the world. However, it is a hugely sought-after one. I think the majority of us long to be a wife someday. More so the idea, I'm sure. Being spoiled or spoiling. Cute trips and pics. Mrs over Ms. and the other cute and fun stuff that could come with it. However, I think we often fail to realize that "wife" is not just a role or title, but it is also a call! A call to a woman to help, respect, submit, and follow.

Now, some of us would equate those words to curse words. And they can sometimes feel that way, but not when the call is answered over the cute idea. Scripture articulates, *"A man who finds a wife finds what is good and receives favor from the Lord!"* Proverbs 18:22. I don't know a lot, but I do know that a man favored by the Lord is a man worth being married to. But there's a prerequisite, him finding a WIFE. So, in being a wife or desiring to become one, the question is, are you living up to the call? The call is first being lived up to in our relationship with the Lord! We should respect, submit, and follow the Lord as well! Why? Because a reflection of our relationship with the Lord will be lived out in every relationship in life.

Our connection with God is never-ending and should always serve as the head of our relationships, especially marriage. God first chose us (Ephesians 1:4), and it is biblical for us to be found and not do the finding; that is God's divine design. So, I pray that in your time alone with the desire, living up to the call, or even being on your way, you are steadily allowing the Lord to work in your heart and prune the things that can potentially cause havoc or disarray in relationships. By no means am I saying only concern yourself with becoming the perfect wife; however, I am saying a good wife is a steadily progressing woman. A woman who knows her worth stands on the foundation of the Word of God and walks graciously in humility. Every footstep is in faith as favor follows closely behind, grasping at the soles of her feet. Whether you're single, married, engaged, or dating, it is so important to know who God created you to be, and that is a beautiful treasure that a man is graced to find and is then seen favorably in the eyes of God.

Pray:

"Dear Lord, I am thankful for the expectations You set for me and for Your word for steadily holding me accountable. Help my heart to stay in a place of humility so that I can always be open to ways to grow in You that will reflect in my relationships. I pray to stay in Your word so that I can grow in wisdom and know my worth. In Jesus' name. Amen."

Push:

1. Do you desire the role of "wife" someday? If you are already a "wife," do you still desire the role?

2. What are some areas in future or current relationships where you can better reflect the character of Christ to serve the relationship that you desire better?

Praise Report:

Describe a previous or current season you witnessed that became better because of wisdom from your relationship with the Lord.

Proclaim:

> *"I am becoming the best woman I can be because I know my Creator defines my worth, and I am created in the image of God!"*

Day 14

Watch Your Mouth

*"Kind words are like honey— sweet to the soul
and healthy for the body."*
Proverbs 16:24 NLT

Every now and then, we all may get a bit of a sweet tooth, some of us more than others. Usually, the sweet treat we crave at the moment is so good to us but not so good for us. We partake in the dessert and, oftentimes, feel guilty about it a little later. It would be great if sugar and honey were created equally! Honey makes things a whole lot sweeter and is actually a lot better for us. Unlike sugar, which has pretty much no nutritional benefits and is just good for the moment. In the verse, Solomon compares words to honey! "Good for the soul and body," he shares. See, good words feel good to us and to the people to whom we say them. However, sometimes our words can be a tad more like sugar, fitting at the moment but over time causing disappointment to yourself and damage to the other person. We allow anger or challenging moments to create false truths in our hearts that can, in turn, make us spew harsh words to people that we love or are called to love. One of the greatest lies ever told is, "Sticks and stones may break my bones, but words can't hurt me!"

"If you claim to be religious but don't control your tongue, you are fooling yourself, and your religion is worthless."
James 1:26

The father of lies had to come up with that one because the devil is a lie! Wounds have the unique ability to heal naturally, but hearts have to be mended. The same time we spend saying harsh words to people or gossiping about them can, in turn, be the same time we spend praying for them, about the situation, or self-control to handle it better. Let's practice choosing honey over sugar, allowing the words that come out of our mouths to be more graceful and prayerful. To uplift people instead of tearing them down and share the grace of God one word at a time.

Pray:

"God, thank You for helping me to watch my mouth. It is so easy when I'm offended to retaliate with offensive and hurtful language. Help me to approach things with gentleness and grace, and my conversations or disagreements ultimately create space for love and kindness. Thank You for being my help in Jesus' name. Amen."

Push:

1. Do you find yourself easily angered and reactive? Does it urge you to speak badly to a person or about them?
2. What specific fruit of the spirit should you ask God to cultivate in your heart to help you be kinder with your words?

Praise:

Honor God with praise for a time when you know it was Him who helped you to have self-control in a moment where you wanted to react.

Proclaim:

"I trust God in my heart and in my mouth; therefore, I practice self-control with what I say to and/or about people and how I conduct myself in difficult situations."

Homegirl Notes

Day 15

Get Ready. Get Set. Believe.

"When He went into the house, the blind men came up to Him, and Jesus said to them, "Do you believe [with a deep, abiding trust] that I am able to do this?" They said to Him, "Yes, Lord."
Matthew 9:28 AMP

Typically, when you hear, "Get ready. Get set..." You immediately think of a track race. You can literally see the movement of the runners in extreme anticipation and ready to take off in full motion toward the destination of their victory. I also know that we can do this in everyday life. Hear certain words and feel like that is our cue to take off and go full speed ahead. But in those moments, we are not activating anything but ability. The truth about a good run is that it is all about how you start. Most runners know that if they get off to a good start, they have a better chance of winning the race. The difference, amongst many, in our relationship with the Lord is that it isn't about our start but more about never giving up.

This walk with God is less about the distance and more about the discipline and determination. Discipline to stay consistent in our pace and determination despite the many oppositions that can attempt to deter you from your final destination. God gives us the ability to do, but we lack the faith to believe. We find ourselves running because of the go but stopping when we can no longer see the end. We're never asked to run in the word of God but to walk because our journey with the Lord is one of pace and patience, not haste and hurry.

> *"So then, just as you have received Christ Jesus as Lord, continue to walk in Him..." Colossians 2:6*

In running full speed ahead, we can not truly seek God or even fully experience the things along the way that build our faith to believe in our victory. Think, if a runner were to take off against the opponents with no knowledge of where the race would end, don't you think it would affect the race? Your race to victory may be because you see the outcome for yourself, but God wants your belief in His perfect plan for you. He is asking you to slow down in the man-made race. Go at the pace of His promise. Activate faith in His word, and win the spiritual battle with patience, self-control, gratitude, and belief with endurance as your trophy. (Hebrews 10:35-36)

Pray:

Dear God, thank You for knowing about my heart. Oftentimes, I do things simply because I can, without checking with You, not utilizing discernment. Just going. I pray, Father God, with faith in You, that belief will be activated and that my faith will be made stronger because of Your word in my heart. I will believe in all situations because I have Your unmovable word to stand on as the foundation of my activated belief. Therefore, I'll go only when You tell me to. In Jesus' name. Amen.

Push:

1. How well do you pace yourself when walking with the Lord?
2. How can you slow down and allow God to help you set the perfect pace to keep you aligned with Him?

Praise Report:

Describe how slowing down and truly embracing your time with the Lord has shifted your perspective in the relationship.

Proclaim:

"I pace myself in my constant walk with the Lord, walking with determination and discipline to keep me on track in my relationship with Him."

Day 16

What's the Real?

"Casting all your cares (all your anxieties, all your worries and all your concerns, once and for all) on Him, for He cares about you (with deepest affection, and watches over you very carefully).
1 Peter 5:7 AMP

It is very common to lie in the passive small talk we encounter daily. At the workplace, in a grocery store, to a faux friend, to a spouse, even to a best friend. The insanely routine "Hey, how are you? I'm good, that's good" dialogue that literally spews out of our mouths like a practiced monologue. It's annoying, but we find ourselves doing it because we fall victim to thinking either they don't care, I don't care, or both. What's sad is that the truth is we can sometimes put those same human characteristics on God, so we find ourselves in a very surface-level conversation with Him, lying about our well-being and actual feelings, all to wrap up a routine conversation to say you had it. Regardless of how you may feel, God is consistent in His feelings for you! And that's extreme love, care, and adoration. He longs for real moments with you. He wants to know deeply what troubles your heart and what's living rent-free in your mind. Not only does He want to know, but He also wants to relieve you and remind you that you are not alone in these feelings. Hebrews 13:5

God doesn't desire to hear your everyday practiced monologue; He longs for "the real." The truth is, He already knows the depths of our hearts, so we can't shock Him with our troubles, but He wants to know if we trust Him with our truth. The secrets, the troubles, and our sincerity. You can't get in trouble with God by being honest, but in His presence, there is freedom, freedom from anxiety, pain, grief, worry, sleeplessness, and whatever may trouble you. (2 Corinthians 3:17) If we stop talking to God, as if we have something better to do or somewhere better to be, we can experience this freedom. What could be better than sitting in the presence of the best listener and comforter with an open heart? We all long to talk to someone about our everyday troubles in life. Why not God? We can no longer talk as if we're waiting on a "good job" sticker for a completed work. Instead, we need an honest conversation where God longs to complete His work in us.

Pray:

"Thank you, God, for being a true listening ear to my heart. You desire to hear me, and I am so thankful for that. Please help me separate how I converse in everyday life from how I converse with You. Thank You for being a safe space for my heart and loving me unconditionally despite its many issues. You cover them, and You cover me. I love You, God, and trust You with everything. In Jesus's name."

Push:

1. Do you struggle to talk to the Lord about your feelings and/or struggles?
2. How has today's devotional shifted your perspective on talking to God about the truths of your heart?

Praise Report:

Take a minute to talk to God about some things that have been troubling your heart, and praise Him for how He will comfort you in this season.

Proclaim:

"I love talking to God about my real life and my true feelings. He is the best listener and a true comforter."

Day 17

Control Freak

*"Better to be patient than powerful;
better to have self-control than to conquer a city."*
Proverbs 16:32 NLT

Maybe you read the title of today's devotion and bucked or rolled your eyes because it resonates with you. Contrary to how the term "control" makes us feel, I believe we all can relate to feeling as though some things are better if we do them ourselves. Maybe it's the work project, group assignment, house cleaning, everyday cooking, parenting, the presentation, being the spokesperson, and the list could go on and on. I am not saying that these things can't be reality. I mean, God did indeed bless us with gifts and talents, as well as weaknesses and strengths, but it's very important in a moment of exercising said gift or talent to check your heart posture in the midst. Are you rude about your advice or correction? Are you more of a hindrance than you are helpful? Could you be enabling more than you are encouraging? Are you being more mean than meaningful? Is it coming from a place of control or care? It was never intended for us to be in control! We all need the Lord's guidance, and even if He doesn't desire to control us, He desires for us to have an organic love that will help us practice controlling ourselves. Self-control is one of the most powerful things that we could ever possess, and it is a fruit of the spirit that we can often ignore.

"For God did not give us a spirit of timidity or cowardice or fear, but [He has given us a spirit] of power and of love and of sound judgment and personal discipline [abilities that result in a calm, well-balanced mind and self-control]."
2 Timothy 1:7 AMP

Truth is, we can't really handle it all, despite how good at it we may be. Having to step up and do everything all of the time is overwhelming. Despite the false sense of gratification we may feel in the moment, the glory was never ours to receive. Sometimes, God receiving glory out of a situation looks like us taking our hands off of it. The Lord allows us to exercise the different strengths He has blessed us with, but true strength comes from discerning our when and how. We have to remember to trust in Him for all things. So the next time you step up to " take control" of a thing, check your heart to make sure it isn't an opportunity to play God but one to pray to God for self-control and care for the situation more than a desire to control it.

Pray:

God, thank You for being in control. Truth is, just because I can doesn't mean I always want to or have to. Help me to be more patient and considerate of those around me so that when You give me the discernment to "take charge," I don't want to miss an opportunity to showcase your grace and give Your name the glory. In Jesus' name. Amen.

Push:

1. What strength has God blessed you with that you may misuse to control your environment, situation, and/or people around you?

2. How can applying the fruit of self-control shift the way you exercise your different strengths?

Praise:

Take a deep breath, breathing in and out slowly. Use that clear mind to praise our God for stepping in and releasing you from the spirit of control and allowing you to walk into self-control.

Proclaim:

"I grace myself in the spirit of self-control in all situations despite the difficulty I may face because, in all things, I want God to receive the glory."

Day 18

Spirit Animal

"For God did not give us a spirit of timidity or cowardice or fear, but [He has given us a spirit] of power and of love and of sound judgment and personal discipline [abilities that result in a calm, well-balanced mind and self-control]."
2 Timothy 1:7 AMP

Typically, spirit animals have the connotation of something inside of you or something that you may feel that you admire or potentially aspire to be, but only reveal itself when warranted. By definition, a spirit animal is "a spirit which helps guide or protect a person on a journey and whose characteristics that person shares or embodies." Hmm, it sounds a little familiar! It sounds like a spirit animal similar to what the Holy Spirit is supposed to do and be in our lives. It may feel a little bit more realistic to look at your favorite celebrity or role model and admire them and say that that's who you ideally "become" when you feel your best, but…

1. That is idolatry.

2. You don't know the true nature of the spirit that you're speaking over yourself.

3. It is demeaning to God to proclaim being filled with anything more than what He left to fulfill us.

It is common for human beings to desire things that are tangible and actually feel a little more attainable. We love for our senses to be appeased. We would rather entertain or be entertained by things that we can touch, feel, see, and smell; these assist us in the feeling of something being real.

But God isn't a God who desires to appease our senses; He would rather we act in surrender. By a simple act of surrender, we may find that we truly have everything that we need. The word of God records, *"We show the power of the Lord to other people. It is like God has removed a cloth from over our faces. He is changing us so that we become more and more like him. We show how great God is more and more clearly. It is the Lord who does all this, by the work of his Spirit."* 2 Corinthians 3:18 EASY

You may feel that you do not fully know the Holy Spirit, but the possibility of knowing Him is available to you. We have access to the fruits of the Spirit as it is written, "*... the fruit of the Spirit the result of His presence within us] is love [unselfish concern for others], joy, [inner] peace, patience [not the ability to wait, but how we act while waiting], kindness, goodness, faithfulness,*" Galatians 5:22 AMP

All the amazing things you need to be your best, most beautiful, and courageous self! God knew that life would be a little tough, so we were created with a built-in spirit animal that wants to know, guide, direct, protect, and keep us in perfect peace.

Pray:

God, thank You for knowing me so intricately that You knew that I could not do life alone. Help me to accept the Holy Spirit fully into my life so that in times when I feel that I need a lot more of something greater than me, I'll know that what You've already placed inside of me, all that I need and that knows what's best for me. In Jesus' name. Amen.

Push:

1. Jesus left us with the Holy Spirit as the fulfillment of God's Word and the last part of the Trinity. Have you come to accept and know the Holy Spirit as God in you?

2. Do you have a better understanding of the Holy Spirit now? If so, how can you better allow the Holy Spirit to be your guide?

Praise Report:

Give the Lord praise for never leaving you or forsaking you. Although you may have felt moments of loneliness, that is not true as it pertains to the word of God; God is always with you.

Proclaim:

"I fully accept the work of the Holy Spirit in my life and in my heart, and with Him, I can do all things through Christ who gives me strength."

Day 19

Compare? Beware!

"For we dare not class ourselves or compare ourselves with those who commend themselves. But they, measuring themselves by themselves, and comparing themselves among themselves, are not wise."
2 Corinthians 10:12 NKJV

If we're being completely honest, comparison is a very easy thing to fall victim to, especially with our access today! Although it is easy to do, it's not easy to accept it or admit it. Unfortunately, it's natural; it is only what we do about the natural feeling that depicts what's next. We live in a time where, with the scroll of a thumb, we can look at our "Dream life." And it is really hard not to think of thoughts of wishing that you could be in that place already or trying to work out your now to get to a future that God never gave you permission to. Comparison being the thief of joy is not just a catchy line that's thrown around because it travels so easily out of the mouths of others, but it is a fact that embodies sincere truth. The moment we begin to measure our lives and accomplishments or lack thereof to the next person, we immediately fall short of the call of God on our lives. Your now is your now. Your then will be there but in alignment with what God sees fit for you if you're patient and in alignment with Him!

What if the life of the person you're comparing yourself to looks nothing like what God has for you? Are you upset with God or more trusting and reliant? What is born from comparison is not the immediate key to the next thing but the key to a potential setback because you're not able to look at the beauty of what God is trying to perfect in you. It looks different for everyone, and although it's not easy to live in, it makes it a little easier to accept. Knowing that you are so special to God and that your journey to God is so unique and purposeful that it may take a little extra fine-tuning to get there. I urge you to beware of comparing and walk boldly in the assignment on your life. Our walks are individual and unique to the plans that God had for us. It is more difficult to walk straight on a path if we're constantly looking at the paths of others. The Bible says, *"For a command is a lamp, teaching is a light, and corrective discipline is the way to life."* Proverbs 6:23 CSB Where you are now is exactly where the Lord needs you to be, to do exactly what He needs you to do, to be exactly who you are becoming!

Pray:

God, thank You for making my path to You unique. It can be really difficult to see others living what seems to be the best life, and I don't feel like I am there yet. Create in me a grateful heart, truly filled with gratitude for my now. I want my focus to be more on You than others so I can be happy about the work You're doing in me now; therefore, I can better appreciate my next. In Jesus' name. Amen.

Push:

1. Do you find yourself struggling with comparison? Why?
2. What active step can you take, with the Holy Spirit as your Help, to assist you in no longer suffering with the spirit of comparison?

Praise Report:

Praise God in your now for the future of no longer suffering from the spirit of comparison. Describe how it has freed you!

Proclaim:

"I am free from the shackles of comparison; I am exactly where I need to be for God to do what He needs to do in me."

Day 20

Troubleshoot

"I am the vine; you are the branches. If you remain in me and I in you, you will bear much fruit; apart from me you can do nothing. If you do not remain in me, you are like a branch that is thrown away and withers; such branches are picked up, thrown into the fire and burned.
John 15:5-6 NIV

It is not a great feeling when you find yourself perfectly cozy in bed, feet rubbing together, with your favorite snack, and about to tune in to the current binge-worthy TV show, all to see a "connection failure" screen. Now, you have to be patient while finding the connection issue and troubleshooting to get back to what you considered the perfect evening. It is an extreme disadvantage to lose connection with the very thing that we need to operate and function properly. For you, this may be coffee, a good run, or a nice hardy meal, but the best functionality and what we truly can't function without comes from a relationship with Jesus! Maybe your relationship with God has reached a plateau, and you're feeling stagnant in your spiritual maturity. Perhaps this is a completely new chapter for you, and you're trying to figure out exactly where to start on this walk with God. Maybe you feel confident about where you are with God and love to find new ways to connect with Him on a daily basis.

"Come close to God and God will come close to you…" James 4:8

Thankfully, it doesn't matter how close you may be to Him or how far you feel from Him! A stronger connection to the Lord is something we all can use because despite where we are now with Him, we don't always feel the same. Sometimes, we have questions that we allow ourselves to wonder about in our minds. We struggle with belief, and we wish we could just talk to God and hear Him as clearly as we hear a friend! Faith in God may not be our easiest task, but it is certainly the most rewarding. Whatever our connection issue may be, it is up to us to find it, bring it to the Source for mending, and prepare our hearts for the best and strongest connection we could ever have. Because, unlike Wi-Fi, you may unplug in your own selfishness, bitterness, anger, hurt, sorrow, grief, or misunderstanding. However, our amazing Father is always "plugged in" and ready for a connection with you.

Pray:

God, if I am honest, I sometimes feel disconnected from You. I don't like this feeling, but it can be hard when I'm dealing with a lot of my own emotions and issues instead of trusting You with them. I pray to stay connected to You so that I can know that You are always with me, in Jesus' name.

Push:

1. Have you ever felt that you've lost connection or struggled to connect with God?
2. How did today's devotional help your confidence in your ability to always connect with God? Do you feel better about your relationship?

Praise Report:

Take a moment to thank God for never wanting to lose connection with you and the ability to always be connected to Him.

Proclaim:

"I am always in relationship with the Lord, even when I feel that I am not." He has gracefully never let me go and always meets me where I am."

Day 21

Power Struggle

"We now have this light shining in our hearts, but we ourselves are like fragile clay jars containing this great treasure. This makes it clear that our great power is from God, not from ourselves."
2 Corinthians 4:7 NLT

Power is defined as the capacity or ability to direct or influence the behavior of others or the course of events. Reading that definition blindly further highlights the average person's struggle in life to obtain this "power" because if power is so easily attainable, it could make us feel as though we can have better control over our lives and the things or people that affect it. We can easily begin to completely misconstrue God's desire for His children and this gift. We then use it as a mechanism to be on top, remain on top, and idolize our idea of what power can do for our day-to-day lives. However, if we were to look at this definition from a biblical perspective versus a worldly one, we'd be able to see exactly what God can do in us and through us if we allowed Him to.

"But you will receive power when the Holy Spirit comes upon you. And you will be my witnesses, telling people about me everywhere— in Jerusalem, throughout Judea, in Samaria, and to the ends of the Earth." – Acts 1:8 NIV

Yes, God blessed us and placed inside of us a mighty power, the very power that raised our amazing Savior from death. This power, in fact, as the literal definition states, can direct and influence others, not for personal gain or glory, but as the Holy Spirit lives in us and through us to show people Jesus. The power of the Holy Spirit is not for self-gain or glory. Nor to further our plans that aren't led by God. It can indeed change the course of events, but not for us to receive the victory. Because of our confidence in God alone, we do not focus on the exact circumstances. We have confidence in being equipped alone with everything that we need for every circumstance! We rejoice in God's mighty power that shines through us, as we are confident that God has everything working together for our good.

Pray:

Thank You, Holy Spirit, for living in me and providing a power in my life that I know cannot come from me alone. Help me to continue to act in humility and remember exactly where this power comes from and its purpose. Forgive me for the times that I have attempted to use it for self-gain and glory, and help me to use it better to glorify You in Jesus' name. Amen.

Push:

1. Have you ever found yourself in a power struggle? Why and how?
2. Could you relinquish your need for power, for the power of the Holy Spirit to work in you to accomplish infinitely more than you can imagine?

Praise Report:

Praise the Lord for not only saving you from yourself by dying for you but also leaving in you a mighty power that helps you and strengthens you to do more than you could ever do alone.

Proclaim:

"I am powerful in the kingdom of God, selflessly beside the Holy Spirit's work within me."

/ Homegirl Notes

Day 22

Not Perfect, But Patient

"But God showed his great love for us by sending Christ to die for us while we were still sinners."
Romans 5:8 NLT

The beautiful thing about imperfection is that it will always leave room for growth. Unfortunately, there are many reminders of our imperfections that stem from sin that we willingly commit on a day-to-day basis because it has become a part of our routine. Sin is a discrete bondage that attempts to hinder us from being purposeful. These things almost come as though they are a part of our personality when they are really adopted lies trying to keep us from the peace that comes from closeness to our Savior. Things such as Gossiping, harsh joking, pre-marital sex, overeating, lust, adultery, jealousy, envy, idolatry, and that's, just to name a few. Listen, everyone has the things that they're convicted of doing. The Bible says, *"So any person who knows what is right to do but does not do it, to him it is sin." James 4:17 AMP.*

God holds us accountable for the things that convict us because the Holy Spirit already helps us to be unsettled in the things that don't align with the word of God. The beautiful thing is that the imperfections that attempt to shape our lives and how we live them don't define who we are nor change how God feels about us. Every single thing about us He foreknew. I'm not saying that sin is okay. When you really know Him, it should be our desire and response to turn away from these things! I am saying that despite His knowledge of how many times we'd turn our backs on Him and choose sin, He still chose us. Now let me ask you: if you knew yourself and all of the ways you would essentially doubt God, would you have sacrificed your only child to save yourself? It may be a hard question to answer or even a pill to swallow, but I didn't ask for you to say unkind things about yourself or add another strike to the list of imperfections. Moreover, consider the weight of God's unconditional love for us to be in a relationship with Him. Despite our imperfections, God is patient and eagerly waiting for us to love Him enough to willingly choose Him over the things keeping us from closeness with Him!

Pray:

God, please forgive me for sins I've committed, known and unknown. I pray for the strength to turn away from these things as I draw closer to You. Thank You for seeing me as worthy of saving! Help me ignore the lies and conceive the truth so I can live easily for You. In Jesus' name. Amen.

Push:

1. What is at least one sin that you struggle with that may try to keep you from closeness with God?
2. Write down the lie (the sin(s) you struggle with), then write a sentence that helps you overcome the sin using the truth of God's Word.

Praise Report:

Describe a time when the grace of God's conviction helped free you from sin. How did that make you feel?

Proclaim:

> *"I am free from the bondage of sin; it does not shape me or make me who I am. I am who God says I am."*

Day 23

Sheep's Clothing

"But you do not believe Me [so you do not trust and follow Me] because you are not My sheep. The sheep that are My own hear My voice and listen to Me; I know them, and they follow Me."
John 10:26-28 AMP

Sheep are quite interesting animals, if I say so myself. I think the closest that most of us have come to a sheep is a good Serta commercial, and if you are a sheep wrangler or something, truly, congratulations are in order. No, seriously, I may not know sheep personally, but a commonly known fact about them is that they're not perceived as the most intelligent animal on the planet; however, one thing about them that is quite impressive is their memory. They always remember and know the face and voice of their shepherd. If they are ever to get out of line, the staff and voice of their shepherd quickly welcome them back. I love that Jesus refers to us as sheep because, in all honesty, we're not the most intelligent beings either. We may be knowledgeable, but we're all ignorant of something. We lack wisdom, and partially, that comes from a lack of reading the word of God and actually applying it to our lives. It is lovely that our Savior is ignorant to nothing.

So, He truly knows best! He is the Word of God, and the Word is Him. (John:14). The staff that Jesus uses for us as His sheep guides us and ultimately protects us. It is so easy to become distracted by the things of the world and wander off into possible harm and temptation. It is humbling to be identified as the sheep of Jesus; therefore, we should be proud not to know it all so that we can respond eagerly to the voice of the correction of our Shepherd, gracefully bringing us back to a place of peace in His presence. Being sensitive to the voice of our Shepherd creates an opportunity for Him to identify us, and no one or anything can take us from the hand of Jesus.

Push:

1. How does being identified as the "sheep" of Jesus make you feel? Safe? Secure? Set apart, maybe?

2. Can you identify the voice of our Shepherd (Jesus Christ our Lord), or do you currently have the wrong shepherd in your life?

Praise Report:

Give thanks to God for not knowing it all, for being able to apply the wisdom of the Word, and for utilizing the Word to help you identify the voice of the Lord.

Proclaim:

"I am a sheep of the Most High Shepherd. I know His voice, and I follow with grace and gratitude."

Day 24

Flee From Me

"Get out of here, Satan," Jesus told him. "For the Scriptures say, 'You must worship the Lord your God and serve only him.' Then the devil went away, and angels came and took care of Jesus.
Matthew 4:10-11 NLT

How do you respond to temptation? Do you immediately give in? Do you think about it and come back to it? Or can you identify that it is indeed temptation and walk away? If we're honest with ourselves, the option to have everything we want when we want it is quite tempting. To just think of a thing or even simply ask and have it is quite literally a person living life the exact way they feel it should go. Wants, desires, and even needs are all real and something that we all have, but the ability to attain them all of the time is truly not worth the expense. In scripture, we learned that even our Savior wasn't above extreme temptation or moments of being alone and in a dry season.

"Then Jesus was led by the Spirit into the wilderness to be tempted there by the devil. For forty days and forty nights he fasted and became very hungry." Matthew 4:1-2

We know that moments of isolation, in addition to a dry season, can equal some terrible outcomes if we are not staying connected to God and using them to further our relationship with Him. Every dry season we may encounter doesn't come from satan or is because of disobedience; sometimes, they are a test from the Lord and a true stirrer and activator of our faith. In times of wilderness, our minds can run rapidly, and all kinds of overthinking can occur. I'm sure the enemy has approached us all in extreme need and tempted us with things that sound and look appetizing, but were you equipped to respond? The Word of God says that Jesus didn't respond with a simple "no thank you." But something more potent, more substantial, unmoving, and unchanging. He responded with the Word of God! We won't be able to respond with something that we don't know and doesn't reside in our hearts, so it is our job to be grounded in our Word so that we can stand firm against the enemy's schemes in everyday battles. We have to be confident and ready to recite back to Him what thus says the Lord! It is then, at that very moment, we experience how the truth of God truly sets us free!

Pray:

Heavenly Father, thank You for an unmovable and unshakeable Word. Your Word is the exact foundation that I need in my life to remind me of who I am. Sometimes, reading it can be overwhelming, and I don't always understand. I pray that You help me to have full clarity when reading the Word so that the words are written in my heart and never leave, and I can fight against everything that tries to come against it. In Jesus' name, Amen.

Push:

1. How often do you sit and read/ study the Word of God? Why or why not?
2. Take time today to sit and read James 1. In it, find at least three scriptures that can help you fight against the enemy in tough seasons.

Praise Report:

Thank God for your freedom in Christ Jesus and the fact that the Word of God alone can move mountains and free you from temptation.

Proclaim:

"The Word of God resides in my heart; therefore, I am confident in every season of life. God has given me the power to command the enemy to let me go!"

Day 25

Daddy's Girl

"They are like trees planted along the riverbank, bearing fruit each season. Their leaves never wither, and they prosper in all they do."
Psalms 1:3 NLT

Life certainly has a way of throwing things at us, thing after thing, moment after moment, time after time. I believe the phrase we use for this today goes a little like "life be life-ing!" In this tailspin of events, we don't wish to put our relationship with God on the back burner, but we inevitably do, attempting to juggle everything all on our own. We begin to create the mindset of "if it is not one thing, it's another." Because of this, we become lost in attempting to find our connection with God, failing to cultivate the relationship because of every other thing that is on our plates. We are now lost in the actions of doing, stressing, and worrying. Finding ourselves overwhelmed and overstimulated, overworked and underpaid, and desperate to find balance in the midst.

What if the balance doesn't always look like being able to juggle it all properly, but more so of what is at the core holding everything up? A large tree could appear to be handling all of the branches that have grown on it, but at its very core, it is about to tip over because it is no longer well-rooted. Balance is not about external work but more about internal work. When we find ourselves firmly rooted in the soil of Jesus, we find that it is fertile, faithful, and fruitful. It is for us to make the decision to desire to trust

Jesus with our seed over trusting the world with it. God wants us to know that there is beauty in trusting Him with what we want to flourish. He simply needs us to remember that He should be at our core for everything to flow properly. It truly isn't balance that we seek; it is being. Just being His daughter and trusting Him as our Father to help us navigate through this life, even when it is, in fact, "life-ing."

Pray:

Dear God, thank You for being such a good-good Father. Life is so hard sometimes, and I am really trying. I'm not purposely ignoring You; I am just struggling with it all. Thank You for changing the way I look at it all. Thank You for giving me the strength I need to trust You to help me navigate. It is You that I desire at the core of my being; I will plant my roots in You to grow strong and, from there, be fruitful in everything that I do. And give all of the glory to You. In Jesus' name. Amen.

Push:

1. Do you find yourself struggling to balance all that life may throw at you?
2. How can knowing that you seek "being" over "balance" shift your perspective and put your mind at ease?

Praise Report:

Take a minute to thank God first for being at the very core of you and keeping you even when you felt like you were about to crumble.

Proclaim:

"With the Lord at the center of my life, everything flows properly. I am less stressed and more at peace just being the daughter of God!"

Day 26

Gatekeeping

"And he said to them, "Go into all the world and proclaim the gospel to the whole creation."
Mark 16:15 ESV

In today's society, nothing is a secret anymore. All we have to do is open our favorite social media platform, and boom, a new tip, trick, hack, or secret to seemingly make life a little easier or better, or even our favorite thing more attainable and favorite food even easier to recreate. There's not much gatekeeping going on to the things we really like or want to have, but I do feel there's a lot of gatekeeping happening concerning the love, the word, and the sovereignty of God. Here's the thing: I think it is so convenient that we have more access to more things now, but just like most things, too much of anything can always have some negative effects. Sometimes, this access to all things cultural and cool can distract us from desiring access to Christ. However, in contrast, God is nothing like most things. In fact, He is incomparable!

There's no such thing as too much God! Our sincere enthusiasm to share all and tell others about the many things we love should be the same, if not more, expressed when we talk about our Lord and Savior, Jesus Christ! Being able to express that nothing can separate us from the love of God! (Romans 8:38-39) God saved us! (Ephesians 2:8) God wants to talk with us and keep us in perfect peace. John 10:27-28 should constantly be on our lips in everyday conversation! Just as easy as the other things that we love and are passionate about that are so frequently spun in our everyday conversations. This shouldn't look like beating people over the head with bibles, but more of an innate exuberance to share the good news of our Good Father, which we can never have too much of because he delights in all of us.

Pray:

Thank You, God, for Your love for me, which is not at all conditional. Please forgive me for the times I've watered myself down or been afraid to bring You up in conversation, too concerned about what others would think of me. When You think of me, You think of love and grace; help me to be bold enough to share that with others consistently so that they can experience Your goodness, too. I will not gatekeep You, God! In Jesus' name. Amen.

Push:

1. Have you ever found yourself keeping God from others so as not to make anyone uncomfortable? Including yourself?
2. How can you become more confident in sharing the good news with others so that they, too, may come to know the Lord as you do?

Praise:

Record a time when you planted a seed in someone's heart about the love of Jesus. How did it make you feel to know that they may come to know God like you? Thank God for that moment.

Proclaim:

"I am not ashamed of the Word of God. Therefore, I will make it more of my everyday conversations because I am not ashamed of my love for my Savior!"

Day 27

Empty Tomb

"He isn't here! He is risen from the dead, just as he said would happen. Come, see where his body was lying."
Matthew 28:6 NLT

Here it comes; you can feel it, the long-awaited "Easter weekend." It's time to overthink which pastel color you or the family should coordinate on this time: hair appointments, nail inspiration, and the perfect haircut for the guys. Now, it's time to walk in the church, preventing tears to ensure the best picture after service. And maybe a good hand wave or shout when we're reminded that "He got up!" Yes, He did, in fact, get up, and Easter weekend is truly the best weekend and certainly worth all of the fuss, but only if the fuss is an activation of faith. Not self-seeking. Not for the better outfit this year or the sleekest hairstyle, but for persistent praise and constant reverence for the fact that we serve a Savior who is not dead and, moreover, laid down His life for us because His life could not be taken. It was a choice! He chose us! Matthew 27:50 informs us that although He was beaten to the point of death, He still made the ultimate decision!

"But Jesus cried out again with a loud voice and GAVE UP his spirit." Matthew 27:50 CSB

He chose to give His Spirit for you to know our Heavenly Father at the capacity in which He knows Him, trust at the capacity in which He trusts Him, and glorify Him in the capacity He glorifies him. My point is that the tomb on the day they went to view the body of Jesus was empty. He did not only die to save us, but He got up to stay with us. As the Truth, the Way, and the Light! Dying for us so that we could come to know all the more, God our Father! God is our Redeemer, and God is our Sustainer because He did it all for the Lord our Savior, Jesus Christ! And the same power that raised Him from the dead, God thought enough of us to fill us with it! Therefore, we should always celebrate the resurrection because it is the resurrection that allows us to experience the fullness of life because, on the third day, the tomb was empty!

Push:

1. Do you only reverence the resurrection on Easter weekend? Why or why not?
2. How can you begin to reverence the Lord's sacrifice for you more often? Do you understand the importance of doing so?

Praise:

Today, in a moment alone, meditate on God's goodness and praise Him specifically for the sacrifice He made with you fully in mind!

Proclaim:

"I will honor the Lord in my everyday life because He is truly worthy of all of my praise."

Day 28

Restful Thinking

"I am at rest in God alone; my salvation comes from him."
Psalm 62:1 CSB

Is it familiar to you to be reminded that God actually desires for us to rest? It is my belief that there's possibly a multitude of reasons in which he would desire this for us. One very important would be that if we were to get too wrapped up in what we could be doing or should be doing, there's then no capacity for being at the hand and foot of God and trusting Him to make things work for the good and the glory of Him. As women, it can be more difficult to get actual rest with the many things continuously on our plates, whether it is education or educating, spouses or children, work-life balance, trying to look good and feel good with hormones intervening to throw everything back off again, nail colors, concealer shades, and the biggest of all, hairstyles! All of these things, to name a few, can truly affect our ability to rest, but not just physically, most importantly, mentally. If we take God at His word to place our trust in Him, we could experience peace, creating the perfect space for rest.

Rest allows us to be renewed and further proves that we truly trust God to be our Jehovah Shalom. God of Peace. Taking moments to step away, unplug, and meditate on God's promises helps us to show up as our best selves and take purposeful steps in everything we do. The Word of God says this: "Study this book of instruction continually. Meditate on it day and night so you will be sure to obey everything written in it. Only then will you prosper and succeed in all you do." - Joshua 1:8

Rest doesn't make us weak; although guilt can make us think otherwise, it builds us up, and our trust in God follows! It isn't necessarily the next hairstyle or concealer shade that we have to rely on God for, but more so, God with our whole lives. When God has our yes, and we're allowing Him the space to truly be the Lord of our lives, we no longer feel the need to control or the weight of overwhelm and having it all together. If we practiced this more, I believe that we, too, would feel like David in Psalm 62:1, at peace because we are kept and secure in the sovereignty of God!

Pray:

Lord, thank You for reminding me that You actually require me to rest. I fail at resting sometimes because my mind goes a mile a minute, and I feel like there is always something that needs to be done. Help me to exercise faith and obedience because I know that I need to trust You more than myself so that I can rest and be my best self. Help me to trust You in all things, in Jesus' name.

Push:

1. Do you struggle with resting well? Why?
2. Do you believe faith in the Lord will help you rest better? How so?

Praise Report:

Take a day where you place your worries on the Lord and let your mind rest. Praise God for a true and comforting rest.

Proclaim:

"I put my trust and faith in the Lord so that I am well-rested and can show up for myself and others in the way God would have me to."

Homegirl Notes

Day 29

Holy Boldness

"My eager expectation and hope is that I will not be ashamed about anything, but that now as always, with all courage, Christ will be highly honored in my body, whether by life or by death."
Philippians 1:20 CSB

As women, we sometimes struggle between not doing enough or doing too much. We can be so overjoyed about what we know God is doing in our lives, but we act almost as if we share too much excitement it can be taken away from us. Like, let's not "jinx" it. Luckily, we don't serve a God of luck. Nothing that He does, has done, or is doing can be taken away from us! The only person that can deter us from God's plans for us is ourselves. One way that I think we do this, oftentimes without knowledge, is discrediting the very thing that God is doing or has done. We hold on to this sense of false humility as though we are content with where we are, but we know that God desires more from us and has already laid out the steps for us to go after it. There are also times in our lives when God has us in a season of hiding and being still, but I'm specifically speaking to the season where God is assigning us to come out and go. I realized that we do God a disservice when we do this because our ultimate purpose in this life is to glorify Him. (1 Corinthians 10:31) How can we glorify God with mediocrity born from disobedience? Our false sense of humility actually comes from a place of fear, thinking of the potential of things going wrong in the journey.

Truth is, they will! There will be some no's. There will be some slow seasons. There will be some tears. And there will be some questions. But in all of that, God is still waiting on you! He never stops being good. He never stops sustaining. He never stops loving or comforting. He never stops being God! And your assignment never changed, but gracefully, you did. You became stronger, wiser, more kind, more patient, and better for the exact thing that He has called you to. No more hiding behind your gifts and talents that you know came from God. No more questioning when and how God qualifies the called and not always call the qualified. No more "I'm good where I am" when God is telling you that you have bigger and better places to go to ultimately bring glory to His name! Everyone's bigger and better doesn't look the same, but our obedience will take us to the exact place that God has for us. We have to not be afraid to go boldly in everything He has called us to, set ourselves apart from the naysayers, and trust God to free us of the fears that try to keep us from placing our faith in God to lead us to our fate.

Pray:

Dear Lord, help me to be proud of who You created me to be and all of the gifts that You've placed inside of me. I sometimes hide them because of my fears of failure and lack of faith, but I know that with You, I can do everything You've set out for me to do. I pray that in everything I do, I bring glory to Your name and that through my obedience and boldness, people come to know You as I do. In Jesus' name. Amen.

Push:

1. Are you currently not using a gift/talent that God had blessed you with because of fear of the unknown?
2. How can the truths of God's word help you to trust Him in all things that He's blessed you with so that you can operate in faith and not fear?

Praise Report:

Give God bold praise for the gifts and talents that He has graciously blessed you with, and maybe describe a time when you trusted God and operated fully in them.

Proclaim:

"I am blessed abundantly, and I have everything that I need to do what God has called me to do and become who He has called me to be."

Day 30

No Gray

"But when you ask him, be sure that your faith is in God alone. Do not waver, for a person with divided loyalty is as unsettled as a wave of the sea that is blown and tossed by the wind."
James 1:6 NLT

Today, it is easy to find ourselves wrapped up in the many things that go on daily that can seem completely harmless. We live in a time where people see no wrong in choosing culture over Christ. Witchcraft over worship. Fame over faith, and even "Woke" over wisdom. If I can be blunt, I genuinely believe that God is over it. He desires to keep us, protect us, provide for us, comfort us, and be nothing short of everything that we need. In turn, we have created idols to fill voids that we haven't been honest with ourselves enough to bring to God to fill, and unfortunately, God can't do anything with what we don't trust Him with! This unsure space puts us right back in the garden of Eden, unprepared to answer the enemy of God when prompted with "Did God really say?" (Genesis 3:1)

We love to look at this moment and say what we would've done or wouldn't have, but the truth is, we fail this prompting daily. In the garden, the enemy did three things: 1. He made Eve question God. 2. He lied. and 3. He made them feel as though God was trying to keep something good from them. Sound familiar? I'm sure because his schemes have not changed today, and it is these exact schemes that attempt to keep us in the gray areas of life.

God doesn't lie, and He wishes to keep nothing good from us but to be good to us in the event that we are obedient to Him.

> *"For the Lord God is our sun and our shield. He gives us grace and glory. The Lord will withhold no good thing from those who do what is right." Psalms 84:11 NLT*

God is also not a God of confusion, and He gives clear direction. We only suffer in discernment when we are unfamiliar with the voice of God because we fail to be in our Word long enough to learn it and be still long enough to listen for it. God saw that we were good and only wanted good for us. We experience this grace when we are obedient and don't remain in a place where He is not. He is fully worthy of our devotion, adoration, love, and reverence. It is in these things that we come to realize that He is God and God alone. Alpha and Omega. Beginning and the End. The King of Glory. The Lord our God is strong and mighty in battle. Our Savior. Our Redeemer and our Deliverer. Forever and ever. Amen.

Pray:

God, I admit I've created some gray areas here and there. Faith isn't always easy, but life without You isn't a life worth living. I don't want to live in the gray, but I want to be with You in the space of clarity and true discernment. I pray for the desire to read Your Word and plant it in my heart so that I can discern Your divine direction for my life and never stray away from it. In Jesus' name. Amen.

Push:

1. Describe an area of your life where you may have created some gray and why.

2. Find in the Word of God, where scripture combats the gray area, and ask the Lord to help make it true in your heart.

Praise:

Spend a few moments praising the Lord for helping you to overcome gray areas that brought you out of dark places and into His love and light.

Proclaim:

"I believe in the word of God in my life, and it lives in my heart so that I know how to combat the lies of the enemy and love the truth of God!"

Day 31

Less of Me

> *"He must become greater and greater,*
> *and I must become less and less."*
> John 3:30 NLT

I used to hear John 3:30 referenced in my spiritually immature ears and make a rather peculiar face brewed in complete confusion. In our full flesh and humanity, the natural goal is not to become less. Not at all. We're actually taught to become bigger, better, greater, more and more successful, etcetera, etcetera. So, innately, to become less doesn't sound like something we'd willingly volunteer to do. When John spoke about becoming less, he said his sole purpose was to prepare God's people for the Messiah, the promised deliverer. Many of us wouldn't be up for the job because instead of preparing God's people for the Chosen One, we would be too concerned with why we weren't chosen. We naturally have the desire to want to feel special so that we can receive recognition and praise from the people around us. Although it's natural, it doesn't mean it's righteous. In this exact realization, I grew in spiritual maturity and came to accept this verse in its fullness. We won't be able to understand this until we are genuinely ok with our flesh shrinking and our faith in God growing. It isn't until we accept this verse in our hearts that we can experience the beauty of how it truly changes our lives and alters the way we know life to be.

In shrinking, we give the Holy Spirit permission to grow in us, prune all the things that are unlike Christ, and grow fruitful in everything we do. (John 15:2) With Jesus becoming our more, we experience an unashamed space with God that allows vulnerability, intimacy, and ultimately fear of the Lord! A healthy fear that can't and doesn't desire to operate in this life without Him. Remembering that it wasn't until Jesus felt that God was no longer with Him that He cried out on the cross. (Matthew 27:46) Not the pain. Not the constant belittling or demeaning, but the feeling of the absence of God. We should be unashamed to hide ourselves so that we can experience a relationship with the Lord that will be our strength through the hardest and most excruciating times and will shift our focus to only suffering in this life if we are in this life without His presence.

Pray:

Dear Lord, I never want to experience life without You. I know that I stray away sometimes and can be too into myself, but I pray to fully grasp John 3:30 in my heart. Lord, forgive me for the times in which I have chosen myself over You, and give me the strength to choose You over me. I pray to cultivate a Holy fear of You that will make me never want to sin against You or be without You. You know me better than I know myself. I ask that You help me trust You in that. Help me stay in Your presence, go in life at Your pace, and always trust Your promise. In Jesus' name. Amen.

Push:

1. Have you ever read or heard John 3:30, at first read and/or listen, how did it make you feel?
2. In hopes that today's devotion helped your context of John 3:30, how can you accept more of God's presence in your life so that you experience good fruit in everything that you are and that you do?

Praise Report:

Describe a time when you experienced the fruit of God in your life because of your humility.

Proclaim:

"I take joy in becoming less to experience God in His fullness. Therefore I never have to live a life without closeness with Him again."

Homegirl Notes

Homegirl Notes

Homegirl Notes

Homegirl Notes

About the Author

Tensia Echols, born and raised in Memphis, TN, is married to Jeffery and the mom of a beautiful baby girl named True. Although most know her for her hand in the cosmetic industry as a natural hair care specialist, it is no secret that she loves Jesus and loves to help people come to know Him for themselves. Sharing the Gospel is not at all new to her. After leading many bible studies, preaching and teaching engagements, and unashamed biblical teaching on her social platforms, she decided it was time to bring her love for sharing the Gospel to a more tangible source: her very first devotional.

www.ingramcontent.com/pod-product-compliance
Lightning Source LLC
LaVergne TN
LVHW011614250625
814666LV00033B/371